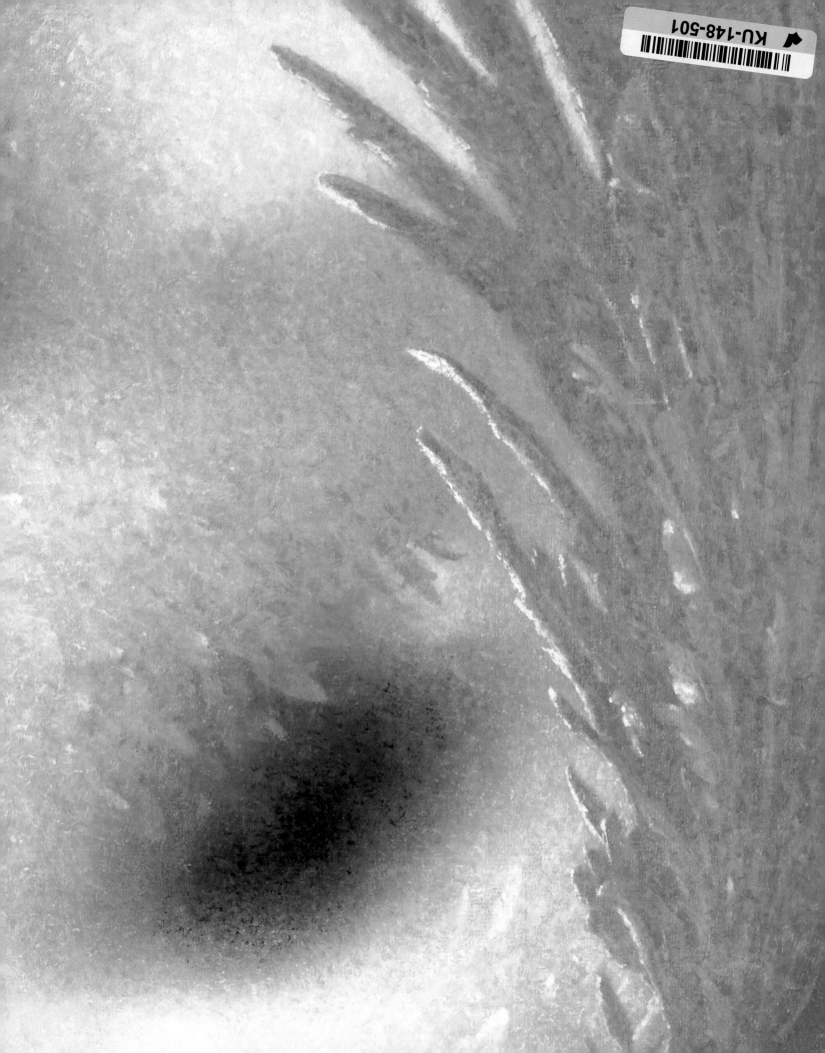

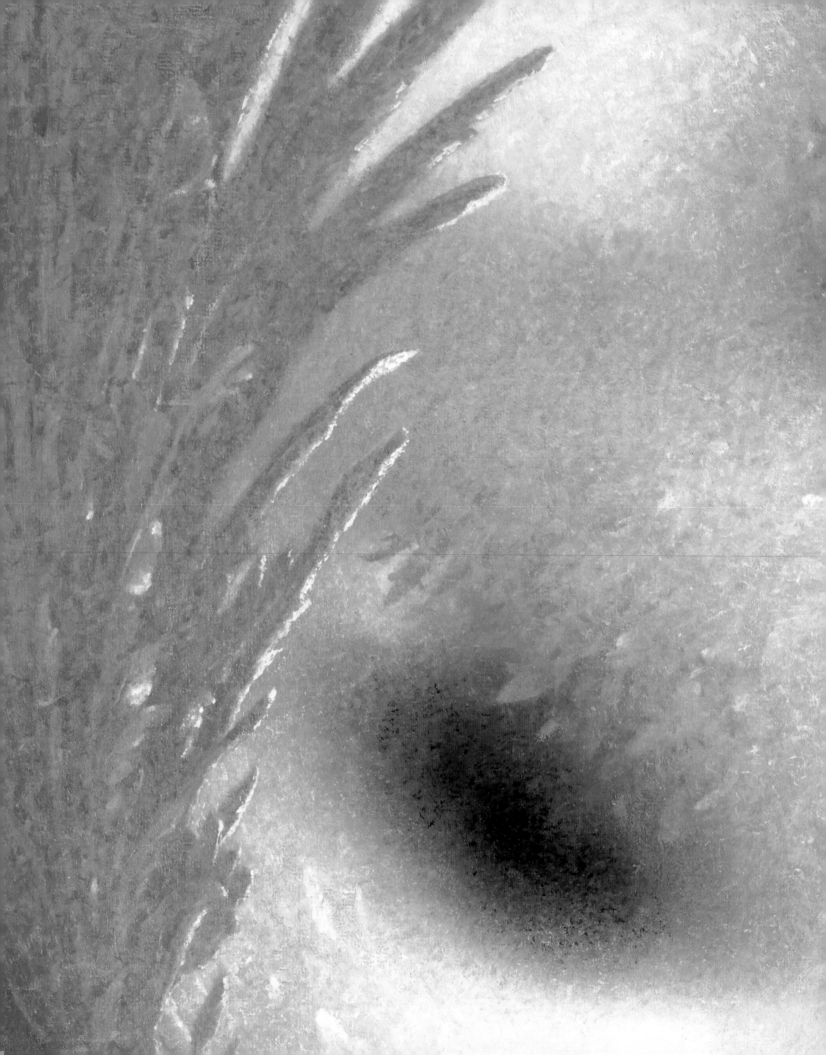

This is the star

For the newly born.
J.D.

To Lin.
G.B.

This is the star

Joyce Dunbar
illustrated by Gary Blythe

Picture Corgi Books

This is the star in the sky.

These are the shepherds watching by night
That saw the star in the sky.

★

This is the angel shining bright,
Who came to the shepherds watching by night
That saw the star in the sky.

This is the donkey with precious load
Trudging the long and weary road,
Looked on by the angel shining bright,
Who came to the shepherds watching by night
That saw the star in the sky.

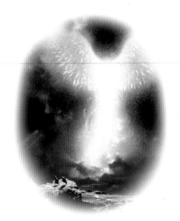

This is the inn where the only room
Was a stable out in the lamplit gloom
For the donkey and his precious load
Who trudged the long and weary road,
Looked on by the angel shining bright,
Who came to the shepherds watching by night
That saw the star in the sky.

This is the ox and this is the ass
Who saw such wonders come to pass
At the darkened inn where the only room
Was a stable out in the lamplit gloom
For the donkey and his precious load
Who trudged the long and weary road,
Looked on by the angel shining bright,
Who came to the shepherds watching by night
That saw the star in the sky.

This is the manger, warm with hay
Wherein a new-born baby lay.
This is the ox and this the ass
Who saw these wonders come to pass
At the darkened inn where the only room
Was a stable out in the lamplit gloom
For the donkey and his precious load
Who trudged the long and weary road,
Looked on by the angel shining bright,
Who came to the shepherds watching by night
That saw the star in the sky.

This is the gold, and fragrant myrrh
And frankincense, the gifts that were
Placed by the manger warm with hay
Wherein a new-born baby lay.
This is the ox and this the ass
Who saw these wonders come to pass
At the darkened inn where the only room
Was a stable out in the lamplit gloom
For the donkey and his precious load
Who trudged the long and weary road,
Looked on by the angel shining bright,
Who came to the shepherds watching by night
That saw the star in the sky.

These are the wise men come from afar
Who also saw and followed the star,
Bearing the gold, and fragrant myrrh
And frankincense, the gifts that were
Placed by the manger warm with hay
Wherein a new-born baby lay.
This is the ox and this the ass
Who saw these wonders come to pass
At the darkened inn where the only room
Was a stable out in the lamplit gloom
For the donkey and his precious load
Who trudged the long and weary road,
Looked on by the angel shining bright,
Who came to the shepherds watching by night
That saw the star in the sky.

This is the child that was born.

This is the Christ child born to be king
While hosts of heavenly angels sing.
These are the wise men come from afar
Who also saw and followed the star,
Bearing the gold, and fragrant myrrh
And frankincense, the gifts that were
Placed by the manger warm with hay
Wherein a new-born baby lay.
This is the ox and this the ass
Who saw these wonders come to pass
At the darkened inn where the only room
Was a stable out in the lamplit gloom
For the donkey and his precious load
Who trudged the long and weary road,
Looked on by the angel shining bright,
Who came to the shepherds watching by night
That saw the star in the sky.

Still shines the star in the sky.

A PICTURE CORGI BOOK: 0 552 528226

First published in Great Britain by Doubleday,
a division of Transworld Publishers Ltd

PRINTING HISTORY
Doubleday edition published 1996
Picture Corgi edition published 1998

Picture Corgi Books are published by Transworld Publishers Ltd,
61 - 63 Uxbridge Road, Ealing, London W5 5SA,
in Australia by Transworld Publishers (Australia) Pty. Ltd,
15-25 Helles Avenue, Moorebank, NSW 2170,
and in New Zealand by Transworld Publishers (NZ) Ltd,
3 William Pickering Drive, Albany, Auckland.

Printed in Belgium by Proost

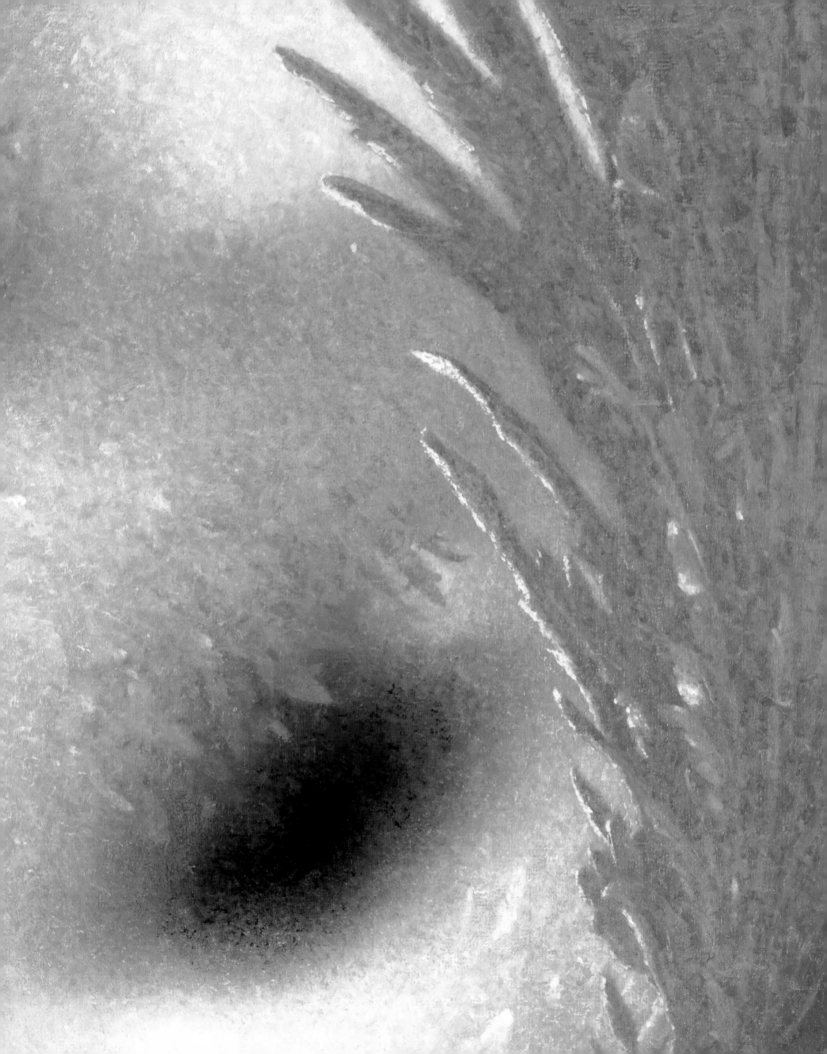

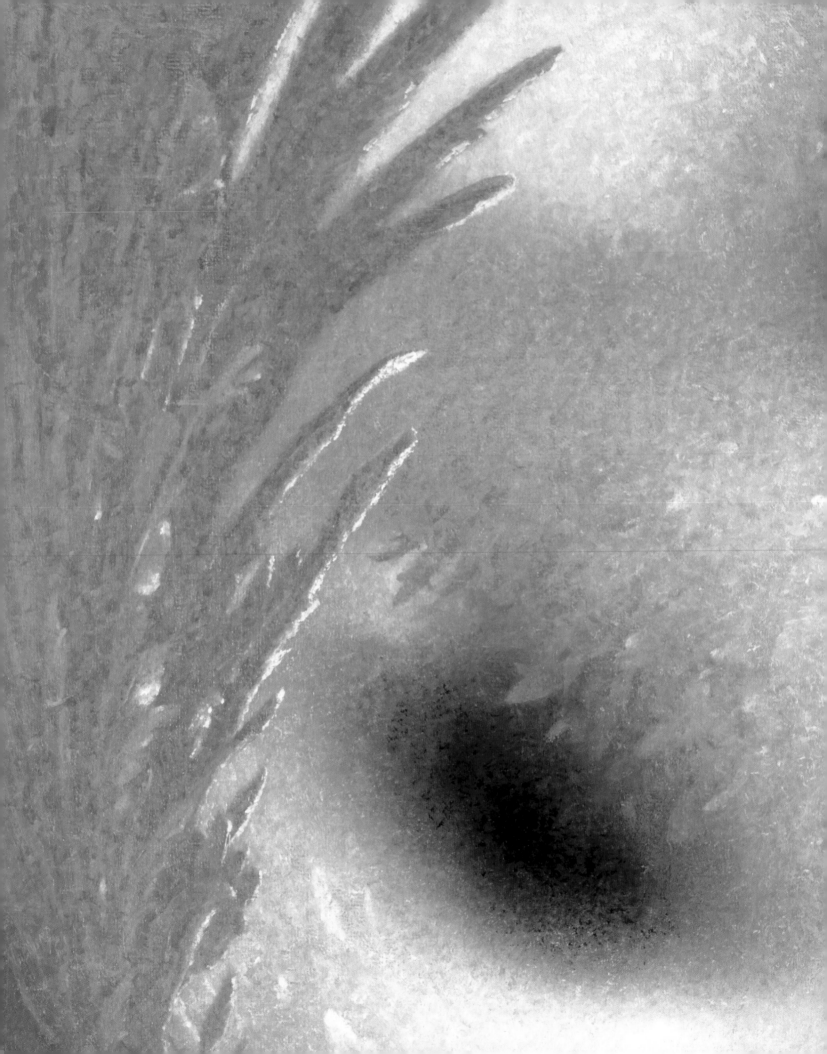

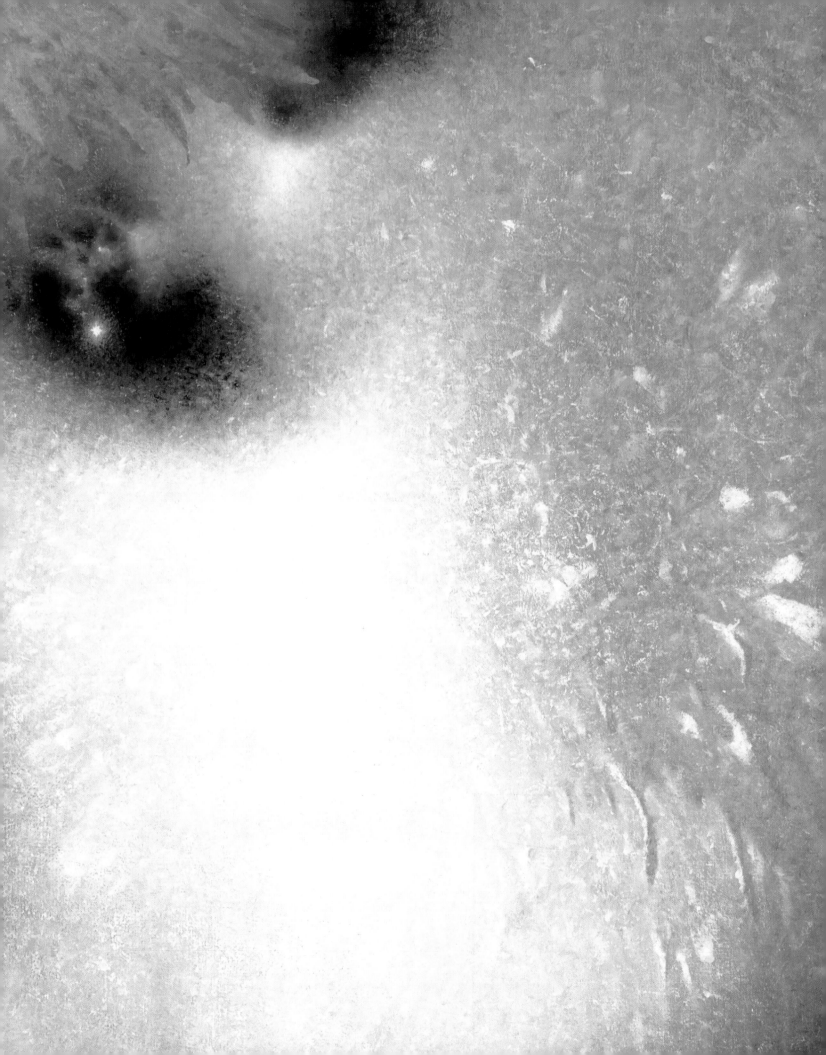